PIANO

CHICAGO

Words and Music by FRED FISHER

as arranged and recorded by

CLAUDE BOLLING

in

ISBN 0-7935-5109-9

HAL•LEONARD™
CORPORATION
7777 W. BLUEMOUND RD. P.O. BOX 13819 MILWAUKEE, WI 53213

as arranged and recorded by Claude Bolling "CROSS OVER USA"

CHICAGO

Words and Music by Fred Fischer

4

Piano

Piano

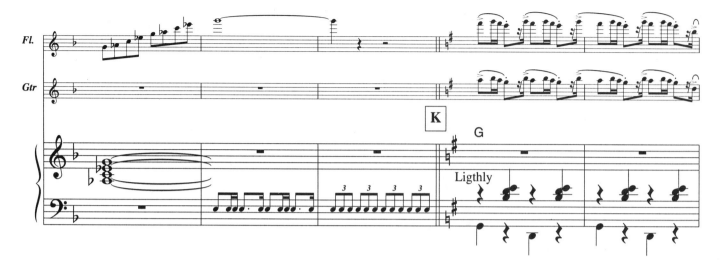

Piano

CHICAGO

Words and Music by FRED FISHER

as arranged and recorded by

CLAUDE BOLLING

in

ISBN 0-7935-5109-9

HAL•LEONARD
CORPORATION

7777 W. BLUEMOUND RD. P.O. BOX 13819 MILWAUKEE, WI 53213

as arranged and recorded by Claude Bolling "CROSS OVER USA"

CHICAGO

Flûte

Words and Music by Fred Fischer

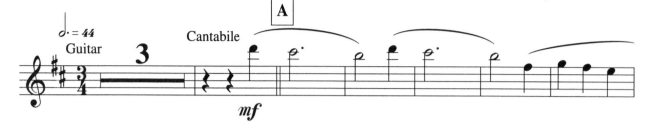

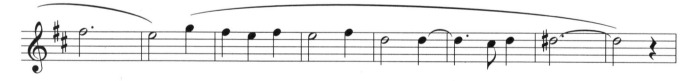

Flûte

Flûte

CHICAGO

Words and Music by FRED FISHER

as arranged and recorded by

CLAUDE BOLLING

in

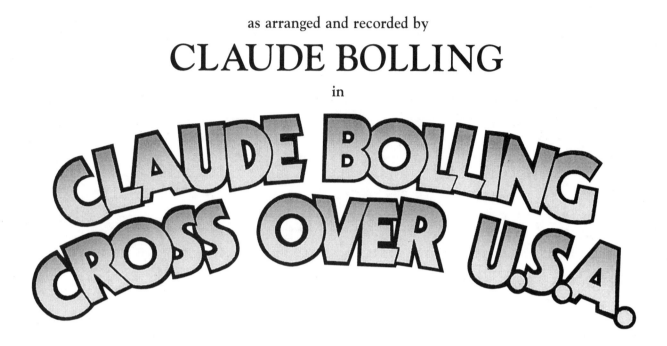

ISBN 0-7935-5109-9

HAL•LEONARD™
CORPORATION

7777 W. BLUEMOUND RD. P.O. BOX 13819 MILWAUKEE, WI 53213

as arranged and recorded by Claude Bolling "CROSS OVER USA"

CHICAGO

Guitar

Words and Music by Fred Fischer

Guitar

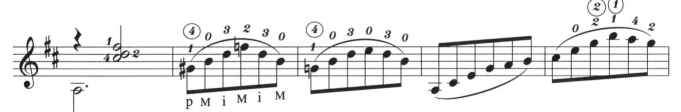

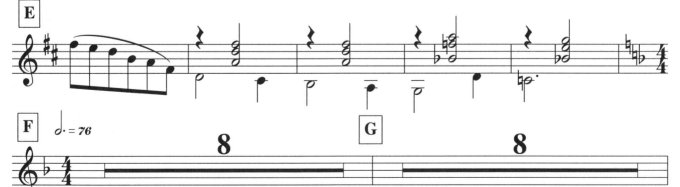

4

Guitar

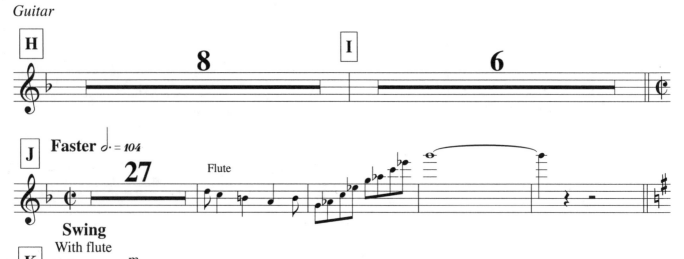

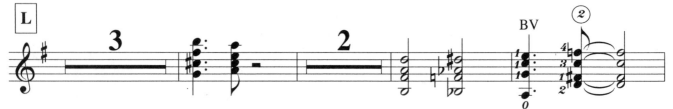

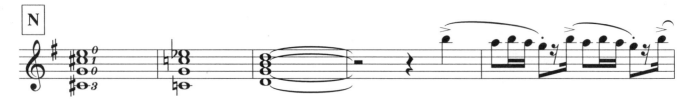

CHICAGO

Words and Music by FRED FISHER

as arranged and recorded by

CLAUDE BOLLING

in

ISBN 0-7935-5109-9

HAL•LEONARD™
CORPORATION

7777 W. BLUEMOUND RD. P.O. BOX 13819 MILWAUKEE, WI 53213

as arranged and recorded by Claude Bolling "CROSS OVER USA"

CHICAGO

Words and Music by Fred Fischer

Bass

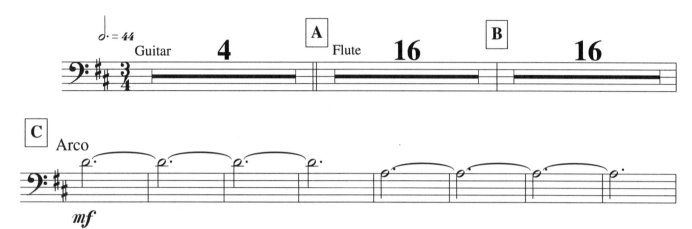

Bass

CHICAGO

Words and Music by FRED FISHER

as arranged and recorded by

CLAUDE BOLLING

in

ISBN 0-7935-5109-9

HAL•LEONARD™
CORPORATION
7777 W. BLUEMOUND RD. P.O. BOX 13819 MILWAUKEE, WI 53213

as arranged and recorded by Claude Bolling "CROSS OVER USA"

CHICAGO

Drums

Words and Music by Fred Fischer

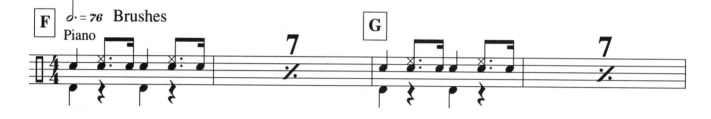

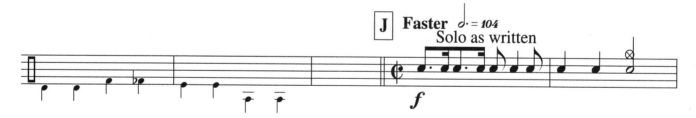

Drums

K Ensemble

L

M

N

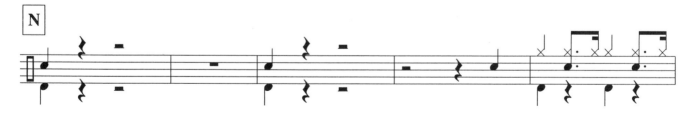

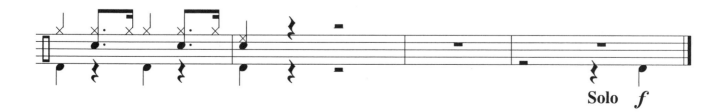